MW00424458

Conversations

on

Tiny Beautiful Things

Cheryl Strayed

By dailyBooks

FREE Download: Bonus Books Included
*Claim Yours with **Any Purchase** of Conversation Starters!*

How to claim your free download:

1. LEAVE MY AMAZON REVIEW.
You Can Also Use the "Write a Customer Review" Button

2. ENTER YOUR BEST EMAIL HERE.
NO SPAM. Your Email is Never Shared and is Protected

Or Scan QR Code

3. RECEIVE YOUR FREE DOWNLOAD.
Download is Delivered Instantly to Inbox

Please Note: This is an unofficial conversation starters guide. If you have not yet read the original work, please do so first.

Copyright © 2015 by dailyBooks. All Rights Reserved. First Published in the United States of America 2015

We hope you enjoy this complementary guide from **dailyBooks**. *We aim to provide quality, thought provoking material to assist in your discovery and discussions on some of today's favorite books.*

Disclaimer / Terms of Use: Product names, logos, brands, and other trademarks featured or referred to within this publication are the property of their respective trademark holders and are not affiliated with dailyBooks. The publisher and author make no representations or warranties with respect to the accuracy or completeness of these contents and disclaim all warranties such as warranties of fitness for a particular purpose. This guide is unofficial and unauthorized. It is not authorized, approved, licensed, or endorsed by the original book's author or publisher and any of their licensees or affiliates.

No part of this publication may be reproduced or retransmitted, electronic or mechanical, without the written permission of the publisher.

Tips for Using dailyBooks Conversation Starters:

EVERY GOOD BOOK CONTAINS A WORLD FAR DEEPER THAN the surface of its pages. The characters and their world come alive through the words on the pages, yet the characters and its world still live on. Questions herein are designed to bring us beneath the surface of the page and invite us into the world that lives on. These questions can be used to:

- Foster a deeper understanding of the book
- Promote an atmosphere of discussion for groups
- Assist in the study of the book, either individually or corporately
- Explore unseen realms of the book as never seen before

About Us:

THROUGH YEARS OF EXPERIENCE AND FIELD EXPERTISE, from newspaper featured book clubs to local library chapters, *dailyBooks* can bring your book discussion to life. Host your book party as we discuss some of today's most widely read books.

Table of Contents

Introducing *Tiny Beautiful Things*

TINY BEAUTIFUL THINGS IS AN INTIMATE COLLECTION OF exchanges between Cheryl Strayed and strangers who felt compelled to share their overwhelming emotions of loss, ineffable sorrows, and somewhat unbearable troubles with "Dear Sugar." Through her earnest yet stern replies drawn from her own grief and failures, Strayed gives some sense and meaning to the chaotic lives of her letter senders and provides them with the hope of redemption. Most of the letters in the book were a selection of "Dear Sugar" columns originally published on the literary website *TheRumpus.net*. Other entries in the book saw print for the first time. These letters were sent anonymously via email to *The Rumpus* or directly to Sugar's email address.

People grappling with great pain come to her seeking clarity and resolution. Unlike other advice columns, which focus on the writer's ordeal or gives responses backed by psychological theories, Strayed lays bare the misfortunes and sorrows she has had to deal with in the past and how she managed to rise above those trials and adversities. For instance, her response to a father mourning for his son's death was: "The strange and painful truth is that I'm a better person because I lost my mom young." Her reply to a 22-year-old reader who was bothered by the uncertainty of the future taps on the universal longing for certainty. "The useless days will add up to something. The shitty waitressing jobs. The hours writing in your journal. The long meandering walks. The hours reading poetry and story collections and novels and dead people's diaries and wondering about sex and God and whether you should shave under your arms or not. These things are your becoming," she wrote. Strayed does not offer clichés or formulaic responses. She gives the right amount of compassion, humor, wit, and wisdom that inspire the broken to be optimistic and hopeful despite life's circumstances.

Strayed provides insights to queries on subjects ranging from romance and love, grief and loss, financial troubles and family matters. Her honesty about human tribulations and the trivialities of life allows readers to feel and empathize, as well as relate to the sufferings of others. The book emphasizes the essence of humanity, faith, and courage to let go and break one's own heart in order to live again. In this day and age when career is equated to life and narcissism to love, Strayed tells us to reflect and value the things that matter: family, friends, and the tiny beautiful things.

Introducing the Author

CHERYL STRAYED IS THE AUTHOR OF THE 2012 NEW YORK Times bestselling book *Tiny Beautiful Things,* a compilation of exchanges between Strayed and letter senders who wrote "Dear Sugar" for advice. From 2010 to 2012, Strayed wrote the column on the online magazine *Rumpus* for free.

Strayed is famous for her New York Times bestselling memoir *Wild,* which chronicles her 1,100 mile trek along the Pacific Crest Trail in the West Coast of the United States. Her first novel *Torch* was a finalist for The Great Lakes Award and was chosen by *The Oregonian* as one of the top ten books for 2006. Her fourth book *Brave Enough* debuted at number 10 in the New York Times bestselling list in the self-help category.

She draws inspiration for her books from unfortunate events in her life and various experiences that broadened her insights on life and humanity. Her parents divorced after they moved to Minnesota when she was just six years old. Her mother was beaten countless times by her father. Strayed saw her mother as a hero as she witnessed how hard it was for her to gather strength to leave him and raise three children alone. To help her mom during her teenage years, Strayed worked as a janitor's assistant at her high school and as a waitress at a Dairy Queen. While juggling these jobs, she still managed to be the captain of the cheerleading team and homecoming queen. Strayed, however, told *The Guardian* that she only pretended to be the "cute blonde person." She said in the same article that she was an "avid reader," who was smarter and more ambitious that anyone gave her credit for. She graduated magna cum laude from the University of Minnesota with a double major in English and Women's Studies. While in college, Strayed's mother died of lung cancer. She described losing her mother as her "genesis story."

Discussion Questions

. . . .

question 1

In responding to a woman who experienced a miscarriage,
Cheryl Strayed shared about working as a "youth advocate" for
white middle school children who were emotionally or sexually
abused. How does the experience of the middle school children
relate to the letter sender's miscarriage? Do you think it was a
good example to choose? Why or why not?

. . . .

. . . .

question 2

When Awful Jealous Person wrote Dear Sugar about feeling
queasy and sad each time she hears of a friend's success, Cheryl
Strayed said a large part of jealousy "rises out of your outsized
sense of entitlement." Do you think most people suffer from
jealousy because of how high they think of themselves?

. . . .

. . . .

question 3

Cheryl Strayed shared some of her memorable experiences in her twenties when letter sender Seeking Wisdom asked her what she would tell her 20-something self. The book is titled after this advice column. How does the title tie up the columns in the book?

. . . .

. . . .

question 4

When letter sender WTF asked Dear Sugar the question, "WTF?"
because he felt like it applies to everything every day, Cheryl
Strayed challenged him to ask better questions. What message
about life is Strayed trying to convey?

. . . .

· ·

question 5

Cheryl Strayed advised aspiring writer Elissa Basist to "write like a motherfucker" and began with a quote by Flannery O'Connor: "The first product of self-knowledge is humility." How did Strayed relate humility with writing as a craft?

· ·

. . . .

question 6

Past failures in a relationship and the fear of commitment are hindering letter sender Johnny from taking romance to the next level. Cheryl Strayed advised him to "hit the iron bell like it's dinner time." What was the "iron bell" alluding to?

. . . .

. . . .

question 7

How do you make amends with the sexual past of your present partner? In the column "Romantic Love is not Competitive Sport," Cheryl Strayed tells the letter sender that it should be gratitude instead of jealousy, insecurity, and fear that she should be feeling. Based on Strayed's advice, how can self-introspection help in fixing relationships?

. . . .

question 8

In the "Magic of Wanting To Be," Cheryl Strayed talks about the life of Cary Grant and how he was able to transcend from his dark past and become a charismatic movie star. Why is it important to present not just our brokenness but also our strengths to the person we want to date?

. . . .

question 9

In the column, "The Ecstatic Parade," letter sender Suffocated
was torn between his family and his gay partner. What can you
say about Cheryl Strayed's concluding note: "This is who I am
even if you'll crucify me for it. Just like Jesus did"?

. . . .

question 10

Cheryl Strayed drew from her own experience when responding to the letter sent by Oh Mama on child support. Although Strayed had a strained relationship with her father, her mother never spoke an ill word about him to her and her siblings. Why is it important not to badmouth a father to his children?

. . . .

. . . .

question 11

In the column "Icky Thought Turns me on," Cheryl Strayed advised letter sender Aching to Submit to play something similar to "Mary Worth." What do you think is the logic behind that?

. . . .

. . . .

question 12

Sacred and Confused confided to Dear Sugar because she no
longer loved her boyfriend of six years, but she was afraid of
being alone and never finding someone who measures up. This
reminded Cheryl Strayed of her own story back when she was a
coffee girl and married to a man she loved. The encounter with a
woman with a bundle on her head made her realize that she no
longer wanted to stay with him. What does the bundle on one's
head mean in this column?

. . . .

                                                              .

question 13

In the column "The Woman Hanging on the End of the Line," Cheryl Strayed pointed out to letter sender, Mourning and Raging, that she should not concentrate her anger on her husband's other woman. Do you think this is an effective way to heal?

question 14

Cheryl Strayed draws from her own experience when giving advice. Do you think using the pseudonym Sugar helped?

question 15

Tiny Beautiful Things is a compilation of columns about topics ranging from professional jealousy to heartbreaks. Overall, what insight did Cheryl Strayed provide readers with?

. . . .

. . . .

question 16

Tiny Beautiful Things sold 100,000 copies, according to Bookscan. What separates this book from other online columns that did not do well in print?

. . . .

. . . .

question 17

HBO has announced its plan to air a drama series based on Cheryl Strayed's *Tiny Beautiful Things.* Do you think the series would have the same cult following as the book and the online column?

. . . .

. . . .

question 18

Reviews published on *Thought Catalog*, *The Huffington Post* and *The Guardian* regard Cheryl Strayed's *Tiny Beautiful Things* as "life-changing," "a gift," and "addictively, breathtakingly great." What do you think makes this self-help book special?

. . . .

question 19

Tiny Beautiful Things debuted at No. 5 on *The New York Times* Best
Seller List and some readers confess buying multiple copies to
give away to their friends. Why do you think people still buy this
even though they can easily access them online?

. . . .

. . . .

question 20

Cheryl Strayed is praised for her unique approach in helping others sort out their problems. What do you think of Strayed's style?

. . . .

FREE Download: Bonus Books Included
*Claim Yours with **Any Purchase** of* Conversation Starters!

How to claim your free download:

4.   LEAVE MY AMAZON REVIEW.
You Can Also Use "Write a Customer Review" Button

5.   ENTER YOUR BEST EMAIL HERE.
NO SPAM. Your Email is Never Shared and is Protected

Or Scan Above

6.   RECEIVE YOUR FREE DOWNLOAD.
Download is Instantly Delivered to Inbox

. . . .

question 21

According to the *New Republic*, Dear Sugar is remaking a genre that has long existed. Do you think sharing her own heartbreaking personal experiences contributed to the success of the book?

. . . .

. . . .

question 22

Samantha Dun, author of *Failing Paris,* said *Tiny Beautiful Things*
would "save your soul." Do you agree with this statement? Why
or why not?

. . . .

. . . .

question 23

Based on the website's traffic, Cheryl Strayed's online advice
column "Dear Sugar" attracted readers who read one column
after another, according to *Rumpus* editor-in-chief Stephen Elliot.
What makes her column engaging?

. . . .

question 24

Cheryl Strayed told the *Oregonian* that the TV adaptation of *Tiny Beautiful Things* would be a drama with a lot of humor. What else do you expect from the HBO series?

. . . .

. . . .

question 25

Cheryl Strayed's online advice column "Dear Sugar" and book
Tiny Beautiful Things are popular for quotes like "Write like a
Motherfucker" and "Believe that the fairy tale is true." Why do
you think people can resonate to these quotes?

. . . .

. . . .

question 26

Cheryl Strayed was just 22 when her mother was diagnosed with lung cancer. She watched her mother grow pale and pass away. Why does Strayed refer to her mother's death as her "genesis story?"

. . . .

. . . .

question 27

When Cheryl Strayed was in high school, she was the captain of
the cheerleading team and homecoming queen. As a small town
girl from Northern Minnesota, why were these titles important
for her back then?

. . . .

. . . .

question 28

After Cheryl Strayed's mother died, she made an impulsive
decision to hike more than a thousand miles of the Pacific Crest
Trail from the Mojave Desert through California and Oregon to
Washington State alone. In what ways did this journey change
her life?

. . . .

question 29

The cover of *Tiny Beautiful Things* carries the quote, "Let yourself be gutted. Let it open you." In her exchanges with the letter senders, why does Cheryl Strayed emphasize the essence of self-introspection?

. . . .

. . . .

question 30

In *Tiny Beautiful Things,* Cheryl Strayed's responses to the letter sender are always grounded on her personal experiences from her seeing her mother being beaten by his father when she was a kid, her experiences as a youth advocate, and a writer of heartbreaks and romance. Do you think her responses would be as effective without the personal anecdotes?

. . . .

. . . .

question 31

Sugar gave advice to a gay man torn between his family and his partner. If you were Sugar, what advice would you give him?

. . . .

. . . .

question 32

Sugar gave advice to a woman who had had a miscarriage. If you were Sugar, what personal experience could you share that could uplift this woman?

. . . .

question 33

Sugar responds to a woman who confessed to having sexual
fantasies about father-daughter incest. If you were Sugar, how
would you respond to this woman?

. . . .

question 34

Sugar received many letters and could not answer them all. If you were to write a letter to Sugar, what would it be about?

. . . .

. . . .

question 35

WTF's letter sparks one of Strayed's most poignant responses. If
you were Sugar, how would you answer WTF?

. . . .

. . . .

question 36

Sugar writes a column on advice she would give to her twenty-something seld. If someone asked you what you would tell to your twenty-something self, what would you say?

. . . .

. . . .

question 37

HBO is making a TV version of *Tiny Beautiful Things*. If you were to make a movie adaptation of *Tiny Beautiful Things*, how would you go about it?

. . . .

· ·

question 38

Awful Jealous Person is very jealous of the success of her friends.
What are you most envious of and why?

· ·

Quiz Questions

. . . .

question 39

True or false: The book *Tiny Beautiful Things* was titled after the letter from Awful Jealous Person.

. . . .

. . . .

question 40

True or false: Aching to Submit was the pseudonym of the letter sender who confessed about how icky thoughts turned her on.

. . . .

. . . .

question 41

True or false: Oh Mama wanted to use a leather stiletto to kick her baby's daddy in the groin.

. . . .

. . . .

question 42

True or false: The old woman with a bundle on her head helped
Strayed realize that she was no longer in love with the man she
was staying with at that time.

. . . .

question 43

True or false: Cheryl Strayed used actor Cary Grant as an example on how the letter sender Fear of Asking Too Much can pretend to be somebody he wants to be.

. . . .

question 44

True or false: Cheryl Strayed used to be a teacher to middle
school children who experienced abuse.

. . . .

question 45

True or false: "Write like a motherfucker" was Cheryl's advice to Elissa Basist.

. . . .

. . . .

question 46

How old was Cheryl Strayed when she started to trek along the
Pacific Crest Trail?

. . . .

question 47

Cheryl Strayed was captain of ____ in high school.

. . . .

question 48

For Cheryl Strayed, her _____ was her genesis story

. . . .

. . . .

question 49

During her teenage years, Chery Strayed was a waitress in _____.

. . . .

. . . .

question 50

Cheryl Strayed's mother died of lung cancer at the age of _____.

. . . .

Quiz Answers

1.   False- Seeking Wisdom
2.   True
3.   False-steel-toed boots
4.   True
5.   True
6.   False-youth advocate
7.   True
8.   26
9.   Cheerleading team
10. Mother's death
11. Dairy Queen
12. 45

THE END

Want to promote your book group? Register here.

PLEASE LEAVE US A FEEDBACK.

THANK YOU!

FREE Download: Bonus Books Included
*Claim Yours with **<u>Any Purchase</u>** of Conversation Starters!*

How to claim your free download:

7.   LEAVE MY AMAZON REVIEW.
You Can Also Use "Write a Customer Review" Button

8.   ENTER YOUR BEST EMAIL HERE.
NO SPAM. Your Email is Never Shared and is Protected

Or Scan Above

9.   RECEIVE YOUR FREE DOWNLOAD.
Download is Instantly Delivered to Inbox